ENTER THE DOJO!
MARTIAL ARTS FOR KIDS

JUJITSU

PHIL CORSO

PowerKiDS
press

New York

Published in 2020 by The Rosen Publishing Group, Inc.
29 East 21st Street, New York, NY 10010

First Edition

Editor: Greg Roza
Book Design: Reann Nye

Photo Credits: Series art Reinhold Leitner/Shutterstock.com; cover InkkStudios/E+/Getty Images; p. 5 Liukov/Shutterstock.com; p. 7 Universal History Archive/ Universal Images Group/Getty Images; p. 8 Neil Lockhart/Shutterstock.com; p. 9 Josh Hedges/Zuffa LLC/Contributor/UFC/Getty Images; p. 11 Nomad_Sou/Shutterstock.com; p. 12 maRRitch/Shutterstock.com; p. 13 Jose Gil/Shutterstock.com; p. 15 Digital Zoo/ DigitalVision/Getty Images; p. 17 ullstein bild/Getty Images; p. 18 Gerville/E+/Getty Images; p. 19 kali9/E+/Getty Images; p. 21 maRRitch/Shutterstock.com; p. 22 Everyonephoto Studio/Shutterstock.com.

Library of Congress Cataloging-in-Publication Data

Names: Corso, Phil, author.
Title: Jujitsu / Phil Corso.
Description: New York : PowerKids Press, [2020] | Series: Enter the dojo!
   martial arts for kids | Includes index.
Identifiers: LCCN 2019019281| ISBN 9781725310063 (pbk.) | ISBN 9781725310087
   (library bound) | ISBN 9781725310070 (6 pack)
Subjects: LCSH: Jiu-jitsu–Juvenile literature.
Classification: LCC GV1114 .C66 2020 | DDC 796.815/2–dc23
LC record available at https://lccn.loc.gov/2019019281

Manufactured in the United States of America

The activities discussed and displayed in this book can cause serious injury when attempted by someone who is untrained in the martial arts. Never try to replicate the techniques in this book without the supervision of a trained martial arts instructor.

CPSIA Compliance Information: Batch #CWPK20. For Further Information contact Rosen Publishing, New York, New York at 1-800-237-9932.

CONTENTS

Get a Clue with Jujitsu

The ancient martial art jujitsu focuses on working with the force of your **opponent**, rather than against it. The term "jujitsu" comes from from the words "jiu," which means to give way, and "jitsu," which means art. The goal is to throw your opponent off by using their force and **momentum** against them, rather than trying to match them.

Jujitsu is a great form of self-defense, but it's much more than that. This **grappling** martial art uses a style that often takes place closer to the ground than other martial arts. Jujitsu uses **techniques** created to make an opponent submit, or give in.

Kiai!

Many martial arts focus on punches and kicks. Jujitsu, however, uses techniques called throws, sweeps, joint locks, and choke holds.

Jujitsu matches start with opponents standing up, but often they end up on the ground. The **competitor** on the bottom in this photograph has applied a jujitsu joint lock to her opponent's arm. Her opponent will have to submit to avoid an injury.

Jujitsu's Origins

Jujitsu is one of the oldest martial arts. Its origins can be traced to **Buddhist** monks from India. However, jujitsu truly took shape in Japan, where Samurai used it to compete against each other. These fighters usually wore armor, carried several weapons, and rode horses. They created jujitsu as a way to fight if they happened to be without armor, weapons, or a horse.

In modern times, new martial arts broke off from jujitsu. Judo is a stripped down variation of jujitsu that focuses mainly on throws and sweeps. Brazilian jujitsu adds powerful ground techniques to the ancient martial art.

Kiai!

In the late 1800s, Japanese masters started sharing ancient jujitsu techniques with others. It quickly spread around the world.

Prise et retournement du bras pour charger ensuite l'adversaire sur l'épaule.

Prise et torsion du bras avec coup sur la jambe pour faire tomber l'adversaire sur son poignard.

Torsion de l'avant-bras sur un coup de poignard.

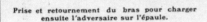

Tous ces coups de lutte sont connus depuis longtemps, Charlemont père les a toujours enseignés et nous avons suivi son exemple mais pas au point d'en faire un exercice spécial. Ces coups sont, en effet, ce que l'on peut appeler des « coups de coquins ». Ils sont en partie connus et pratiqués par les rôdeurs de barrière qui, cependant, n'ont jamais appris le jiu-jitsu.

CH. CHARLEMONT.

Torsion du bras dans une tentative de prise de corps.

Retournement du bras sur une prise de corps en arrière. L'adversaire, brusquement, a saisi le poignet et le bras.

Coup de pied direct sur la main pour faire lâcher le poignard.

Retournement du bras en arrière avec coup de pied dans le jarret pour faire tomber.

Passement de jambe et prise à la gorge pour faire tomber l'adversaire en arrière.

The Modern Era

People practicing jujitsu today keep it modern by creating new moves, techniques, and training styles. During the twentieth century, Brazilian martial artists transformed jujitsu into a new and very exciting form, now called Brazilian jujitsu, or BJJ. BJJ competitions have become major sporting events. The two largest are the Abu Dhabi World Professional Jiu-Jitsu Championship and the World IBJJF Jiu-Jitsu Championship.

In this photograph from 2011, MMA fighter Jeremy Stephens (white trunks) applies a jujitsu lock called a Kimura to the arm of Danny Downes (black trunks). Downes was forced to tap out, or give up, and Stephens won the match.

Mixed Martial Arts (MMA) has become very popular recently. Most MMA fighters need a basic knowledge of jujitsu to have any chance at competing at the **professional** level. This has helped keep jujitsu popular.

Going to the Mat

Throws and sweeps are two ways a jujitsu competitor knocks their opponent off balance. One of the most common throws in jujitsu is the tai otoshi, or body drop. There are numerous ways of doing this move, but all require twisting the opponent's upper body to get them off balance and using an outstretched leg to "trip" the opponent.

A sweep is a technique using your foot to upset an opponent's **stance**. As an opponent moves or steps, a sweep can be used to take their feet out from under them. In BJJ, sweeps are important movements made from the ground, too.

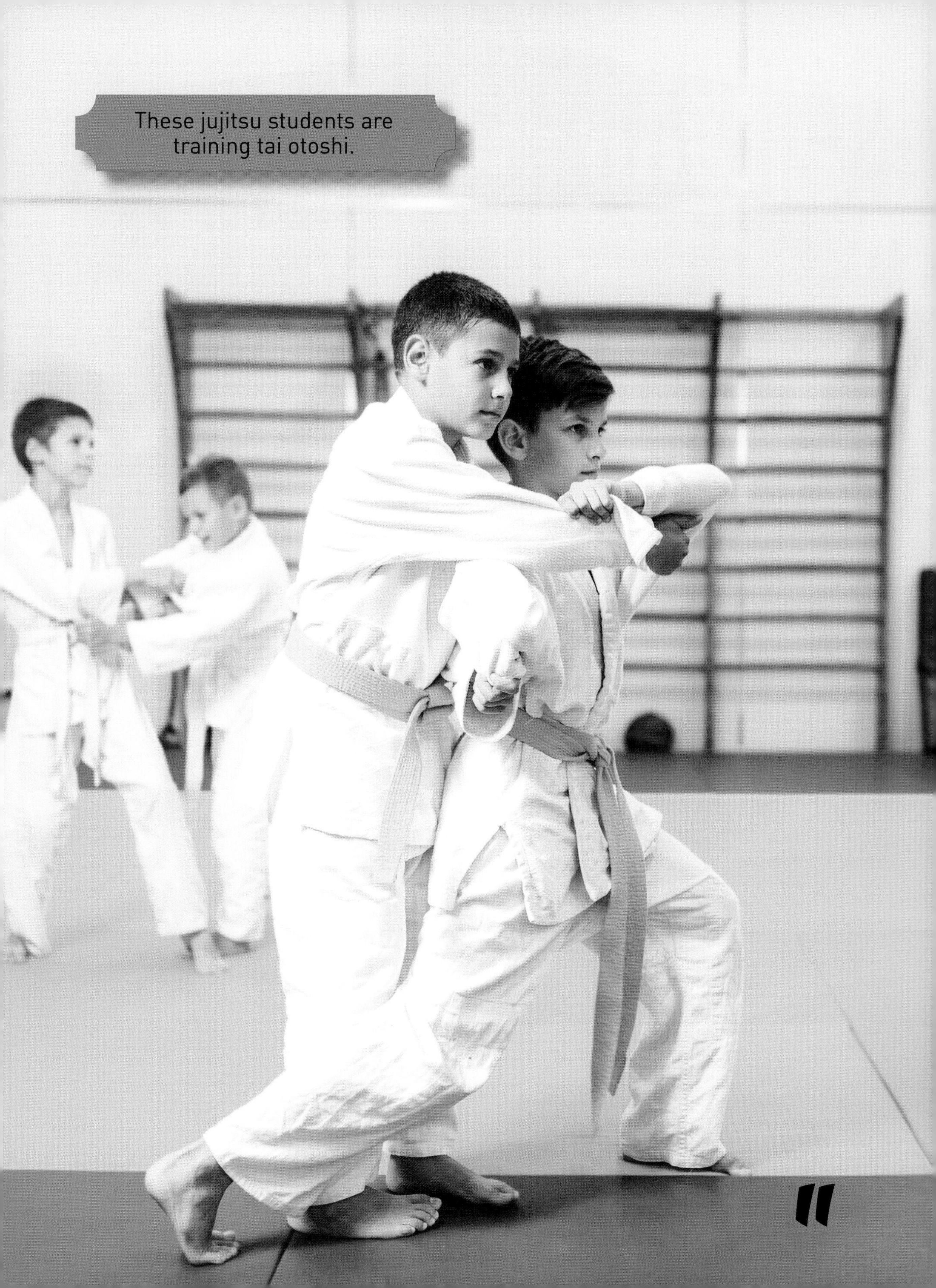

These jujitsu students are training tai otoshi.

Submission Moves

Joint locks and choke holds are techniques created to make an opponent tap out because of pain or a lack of air. Locks place strain on one or more of your opponent's joints, such as wrists, elbows, knees, or ankles. Common joint locks include the arm bar and the Kimura, an elbow and shoulder lock.

Kiai!

Trust is a key part of training. If your partner taps you or the mat, let go immediately to avoid injury. If your opponent can't free a hand to tap, they may say "tap."

These two jujitsu instructors are demonstrating the proper way to apply the rear naked choke.

The rear naked choke, also known as a "sleeper hold," is a common **submission** move in MMA. To apply the choke, you need to get behind your opponent and wrap your arm around their neck. Then, grab your other arm and squeeze!

First Steps

The typical clothing worn for most martial arts is known as a gi. Gis are held together by a belt tied around your waist. These belts have different colors to represent a student's level of skill.

Before entering the dojo, you should remove all jewelry to avoid injuries. **Hygiene** is important, too, since you will be in close contact with others. And if you have long hair, you will need to make sure that it is tied up in such a way so that it does not get in the way of your training.

Kiai!

Dojos are places where it's important to show respect for your instructors, other students, and yourself. Bowing to each other is a common sign of respect in the martial arts.

Colored belts show all students your level of experience. It's important to go easier on people with lower belts than you have to avoid injuries, and to help lower-level students learn.

Jujitsu Training

Jujitsu is a grappling martial art. It can be a tiring activity. To train effectively, you should focus on **cardiovascular** training such as running or swimming. Stretching and breathing exercises help students avoid injuries. Lifting weights helps build strength as well as **endurance** and **flexibility**.

One of the first techniques beginning jujitsu students learn is how to fall properly. Students trip and throw each other numerous times with various techniques during each class. Practicing falling, and how to defend yourself from the ground, are important skills to learn. Once a student can do these moves, they can start sparring, or practice fighting, with other students.

Kiai!

Your instructor can help you learn new techniques and terms on the mat. Many instructors expect students to count in Japanese and learn the Japanese terms for all moves.

One way to improve in jujitsu is to experiment when you are sparring. Just be careful not to hurt your partner.

Levels of Experience

Sparring is an important step in all martial arts. While sparring, students may be asked to go slow and make sure they have the technique right. In time, students will speed up as their level of experience increases. As a student's knowledge and skill increase, they earn new belts to display their level of experience. A black belt is a sign that a student has mastered all the basics of a martial art.

Kiai!

The belt system for BJJ works the same way but is a little different. BJJ has five belts, and it can take many years to reach black belt. Many BJJ dojos use "stripes" on a belt to show smaller levels of success.

More advanced jujitsu techniques can be dangerous for students of lower levels. Hip throws, shoulder throws, neck cranks, and knee locks can all cause terrible injuries. It's important to keep this in mind while sparring.

Jujitsu for Self-Defense

Many people train in jujitsu for health reasons. Some like to compete with other athletes. However, some jujitsu students are training so they can keep themselves safe. Many jujitsu techniques were created as a defense against attacks.

One of the most common attacks in the real world is a grab. Jujitsu students learn how to break free from grabs and to turn the attack back against the other person. For example, wrist grabs are very common in beginning jujitsu classes. Pairs of students practice wrist grabs, taking turns being the "tori" (person practicing a technique) and the "uke" (person accepting the attack).

The tori/uke relationship is important to proper training in the martial arts. The uke allows the tori to practice techniques. The tori is careful not to hurt the uke.

The Rewards of Jujitsu

Training in jujitsu comes with plenty of rewards. Jujitsu techniques have been proven to be excellent self-defense skills. Jujitsu is also a great workout. Drilling sessions and sparring help tone the body and grow muscle.

Sometimes referred to as a "game of human chess," jujitsu is also an activity that sharpens the mind. Jujitsu fighters quickly sift through a long list of moves to try and figure out the most effective way to beat an opponent.

On top of all that, jujitsu is fun! It's a great way to meet people with similar interests. Now that you know about jujitsu, it's time to enter the dojo!

GLOSSARY

Buddhist: Someone who practices the religion of Buddhism.

cardiovascular: Relating to the heart and blood vessels.

competitor: Someone who is trying to win something or be better than all others.

endurance: The ability to do something difficult for a long time.

flexibility: Capable of bending or stretching without injury.

grapple: To grab and struggle with another person.

hygiene: The things people do to stay clean and healthy.

momentum: The strength or force that something has when it is moving.

opponent: Someone competing against another person.

professional: Having to do with a job someone does for a living.

stance: The way someone stands.

submission: In the martial arts, when one competitor quits to avoid an injury or a loss of consciousness.

technique: The manner in which physical movements are used for a particular purpose, such as training in a martial art.

INDEX

WEBSITES

Due to the changing nature of Internet links, PowerKids Press has developed an online list of websites related to the subject of this book. This site is updated regularly. Please use this link to access the list: www.powerkidslinks.com/ETD/jujitsu